Tell It As It Is

Gordon Savory

with Mark Smith

Published in 2012 by FeedARead.com Publishing –
Arts Council funded

A CIP catalogue record for this title is available from
the British Library.

Contents

1

London Life – Late 1940s

Born in 1945, the earliest memories I have are from 1948, three years after the end of the Second World War. At that time, my immediate family was my mother, who I shall call Sally, and two brothers who I shall call Steve, born in 1942, and Bill, born in 1944. I have no picture in my mind of what my mother looked like, likewise my father, who died on my first birthday in 1946.

For our annual holiday, an open-backed lorry would turn up in the street and we would collect together a few pots and pans, blankets and other bare necessities and head off with other families from the same street to Kent for hop picking at harvest time. This was a typical holiday for many working class families from central London. Along with my brothers, I had extended family with me which included half-sisters. One of the men would look after us in the daytime while most adults would be gathering in the harvest. When we arrived at the farm, the various families were taken to different sheds. The provisions for the week, for sleeping, were a few blankets which we had taken with us to lay on top and a pile of straw. The cooking arrangements were an open fire in the field where the hut was and whatever we could put in the pot! I can remember this was a happy time when I never felt out of place as there were lots of other children in the same circumstances.

Tell It As It Is

On returning back to Lambeth, life seemed to continue much the same. Our daytime activity was playing on many of the bombed ruins and frequently being told off by policeman and the older people in the area. Our accommodation in Lambeth was an apartment with a central living room cum dining room cum kitchen and bathroom! The living room had an open fire and an old grey gas cooker and gas light. There was a bedroom either side of the living room, one in which I and my brothers slept, sharing an old double bed, and the other room was my mother's. When other children came from various half-sisters' families they would have to share with us in our double bed. It was a happy life, the only life I had known, so I was very contented.

The first feelings of sadness were to follow at the age of four when, unbeknown to me at the time, my mother was suffering from cancer. She died when I was four and a half. I've no memory of the funeral or how I reacted at that time, but I believe I was quite naughty!

Being orphaned, my brothers and I were initially rescued by our half-sister, who I shall call Phoebe, who was recently married and around twenty years old. She had a toddler to look after in addition to me and my brothers. She really struggled to take care of us despite good intentions. She gave us free reign around the neighbourhood which was a new experience for us and resulted in lots of incidents! For example, I would frequently stand between the tram lines and hold my hand up like a policeman so the tram could not pass without running me over. Fortunately, I'm still here to tell my story! One of my pastimes with other boys from the street was to wait until the local church congregation were in prayer on their knees whilst someone would hold the door open. I would then throw half a house brick down the aisle! The previous year at this same church when I was aged three and a half, I noticed some very pretty flowers on the altar and climbed on the altar to retrieve them for my mother who I thought would appreciate them much more. I had just arrived home with the flowers to hear banging on our door. It was the local priest asking me to return the flowers and it was unanimously agreed by the family that I should promptly comply! When entering the church with the priest, he took me to the altar and made me kneel down and say a prayer to say I was sorry. But I wasn't sure what I was saying sorry for and still wanted to take the flowers away with me!

Whilst with Phoebe another game we would play would be to trick the tram lady who was responsible for carrying out the driver's instructions to change direction. She would have to get off the tram, put a long pole up near a wire and pull it so that the tram could go in a different direction. Then she would have to return to the tram and press the bell to give the "all clear" to the driver. Whilst she was in the process of giving the "all clear," I would sit on someone's shoulders so I could reach the pole and pull it once more so the tram would continue in the same direction instead of the intended direction. Many words were shouted at us which are better not mentioned, and with much laughter all around! Very few people in our social circle owned a telly in those days so entertainment came through our own means.

My learning experiences in life were often attained in testing what I'd been told and discovering the wisdom of it after making mistakes at the expense of others. An example of this is, at the age of four, my elder brother mentioning that when cats jump from a height, they will always land on their feet. So I immediately thought I'd put this to the test. I picked up next door's tomcat and posted him through the bedroom window of our third floor apartment. On realising the cat was motionless on the ground, I felt very sorry for the cat, but, being so young, I did not appreciate that I was the cause of this unnecessary loss! Understandably, my neighbour was not best pleased but at a later time gave me a sweet.

Another experience at that time related to delivery of milk in our street which was done by horse and cart. When we were playing in the street, we observed that the milkman would bring the horse to a halt with the word "Whoa!" On returning, after delivery, he would use the words "Gidee-up-there!" to set the horse on its way to the next drop off point. After learning how to mimic the milkman's voice we had great fun in setting the horse on its way before the milkman returned with his empty bottles. At this point, we learned words from the milkman that, on entering school, I discovered were not acceptable!

2

Life in Care

Soon I was about to lose all sense of security as Phoebe was finding us too much to look after, three boisterous boys amongst the dangers of central London and very poor living conditions. I and my brothers were finding life difficult. These were uncertain times for three young boys. With the financial, emotional and physical demands becoming too much for Phoebe and her husband, a decision was made to seek help and we were put in care by the London County Council a short period after my mother's death. My mother had made a request when she was dying that both I and my two brothers would be kept together through our childhood. This request was complied with throughout our time in care.

We were taken into care by an organisation called Waifs and Strays (later known as The Children's Society). My first shock I was when I was introduced to a man called "God". The name sounded easy to say, so no problems there! We were sent to an orphanage in Devon, many miles from London in a village local to Tiverton. This was a complete contrast to life as I had known it. There was a beautiful canal with lilies, swans and their young – a really picturesque place. There was a very difficult transition and I yearned to return to my roots in central London. That was home to me.

In the two years I spent in Devon, life seemed quite happy as many people at this time were trying to establish a new life after the Second World War. One of the first major shocks was my first day at school. It was a non-starter! To have to sit still for short periods of time was almost impossible for me after living in central London. The tranquillity of the countryside and an encounter with nature in its full beauty was such a contrast to the life I had known before. There were many kind and understanding people around me at this time. However, I was unable to understand the enormity of what had taken place in my life and was ill prepared for what lay ahead. Life was never to be the same again.

Towards the end of my first two years in care, we were transferred to Lancashire. This was another contrast in both weather conditions and lifestyle which was much harsher in the north (It's grim up north!). I was now aged seven and my schooling was suffering badly because of my emotional insecurity and instability with my relationships with older people. This orphanage was much smaller than the one in Devon holding about twenty to twenty-four children at any one time. However, it seemed much harsher. The tears would flow at night and a sense of bewilderment would be present for many years to come. Concentration became very hard at school and I was unable to attain any reasonable standard of education. Often as local orphans, we were easy targets for other children. I soon learned ways of defending myself, whether they were good or bad as I found punishment very hard to take, especially when many allegations made against me at school were unfounded.

The cane was often used for poor performance in school. It became very apparent that my literary skills were not progressing as expected although I would really try for many hours, often in secrecy as I felt very demoralised that I was unable to progress and was feeling very inadequate as a pupil at school. I compensated for these feelings of inadequacy with boldness of character and living dangerously as you will begin to see as I took up employment. One of the more humorous examples of my schooling was regarding my reading ability which, at that particular time, was one of the lowest in the school. At around age twelve, I bought my yearly school report home which covered my position in class for each subject. When it came to reading, I had been marked as third in class. This went down with great delight, both from the people in charge of the orphanage and the vicar of the church I attended. On reading the report, the vicar put his hand in his pocket and pulled out two shillings which he gave me with a big grin on his face and patted my head. Two months later he was to find out that because of my inability to read I had been put into a class of three! I think for the first time he became speechless (but I did enjoy the two shillings which were used to purchase lots of lovely sweets). Thank you vicar, He's a good God! On a more serious note though, I think the authorities in The Children's Society were quite concerned about my lack of progress and my behaviour towards authority was becoming more resentful.

In school, I was often penalised for not attaining the expected academic standards by abusive physical and psychological punishments. For example, quite regularly I would be asked to stand up in front of the class and read and write on the blackboard which would humiliate me and I would become defiant because I knew they were aware of my situation. Therefore, I would often receive the cane for insolence but was unable to explain or reason out within myself the reason why I was unable to read. I wanted to learn about life and the beauty of things and have a greater understanding of the country I lived in and far beyond. I had no understanding of my vulnerability in pursuing this dream.

In the orphanage, we were made to feel very blessed that we had food to eat and a place to stay and were reminded that this had all come about because of charity. Yet we felt the tension of the fact that many children were enjoying a much better life than we were, with loving and stable families, home comforts and a bright future ahead of them. The orphanage had a high turnover of workers who were known to us as "Aunties" or "Uncles." Another difficulty that arose was that the female staff members were very young and on entering puberty, we found it hard to interact with them or discuss any difficulties we were experiencing. With little time for quality relationships to develop, we struggled with trusting people and being taken seriously. This was to continue for many years of my life – who could I trust?

It was policy that when a person in care became working age, they would leave the care of the orphanage. As Steve turned fifteen, the working age of that time, he duly returned to London. Phoebe had moved to a larger property and Steve took up lodgings with her and her family which had then increased to about four children. Feeling the loss of my brother, I felt more isolated than ever. It seemed that my carers couldn't understand the trauma I was going through.

Discussions were held with the appropriate authorities of the possibility of us being relocated south, but we were not informed of this at the time. On reflection, I can see the tremendous difficulties that the carers faced including low pay, long hours, shortage of staff, dealing with children from traumatic backgrounds and hardships faced in the aftermath of the war. Within myself, I started to deteriorate emotionally because of the uncertainty of my life and I had a growing fear of how I would cope with life in the outside world with very little support. The way I handled this was to put on a bold determination to succeed against the odds and I wanted to try my luck at every opportunity that came my way.

3

Opportunity Knocks

A significant opportunity came up around age twelve when I joined the Sea Cadets. I enjoyed all the activities I took part in which included sailing, learning to work as part of a team and being in close contact with water. I had always enjoyed swimming from an early age but it sure was cold up north! I had started to toughen up physically and learned to take a few punches and land a few myself. This was very much the way of life in the north of England in the late 1950s. Life in the orphanage was very regimental, routine and discipline had become the norm for me. For example, one of our tasks at the age of ten onwards was to work in a team of five fellow orphans and shovel three tonnes of coke using buckets into the boiler house to heat the house and water supply for the week. This was carried out in all weathers: snow, rain – eh... it's cold up north! But it was helping me gain physical strength which would be of value later in life.

So I fitted in well with the Sea Cadets with their Royal Navy principle of carrying out orders and looking after your fellow comrades. It was a bonding process both within the orphanage and within the Sea Cadets. One of the tasks I least enjoyed was peeling all the potatoes required for the next day using a potato peeler and often getting blisters. I hadn't got tough enough yet to enjoy this task! As we drew nearer to bonfire night, we would cut trees down to build a big bonfire and the staff would make treacle toffee and jacket potatoes would be cooked. On the evening of the 5th November, we would enjoy the bonfire, the fireworks that had been given us and the delicious food prepared.

When I was twelve, the staff at the orphanage saw that I needed some individual literacy tuition in a small family environment. I was introduced to a family in which, unbeknown to me, one of the parents was a school teacher. I couldn't understand how this would help me because the contrast of environment was uncomfortable and it takes time to establish trustful relationships. I felt I could never meet their expectations, that I had nothing in common with my surroundings other than the desire to have a good time. Silence was often the result of this from both sides. The family became frustrated at my lack of progress and eventually gave up, but I felt this was unfair because I was not given enough time to adjust. I felt there were good intentions at all times from these people but it was very much a case of trial and error in whether or not they could help me.

Later at the orphanage, a couple from Yorkshire, who I shall call Mr and Mrs Brown, were introduced to Bill and me. We established a relationship with them over a period of about two years. They enjoyed camping in the Lake District and wished to help by taking two older children with them on their holidays. I got on much better with these people. There were lots of activities; climbing mountains, riding horses, swimming lakes and camping in fields with just a tent and primitive cooking conditions. The latrine consisted of digging a hole in the woods and covering up after use. All water was drawn from the local stream.

Opportunity Knocks

I didn't look upstream when drawing it but I was aware that it might have been fouled by cattle or anyone relieving themselves into it – the sort of thing I might have done! The water, however, did taste good. As this holiday drew to a close, it became apparent that I was fretting unlike ever before. I did not wish to return to the orphanage as Bill had reached working age and I knew I would be on my own. I found the thought of being there without Bill unbearable. The staff in charge had changed before we had gone on holiday and the new staff had made it clear that they did not want me to stay in that particular home. The only way to describe my feelings at the time was "despair." There seemed no way out. As my time on the holiday was drawing to a close, the couple encouraged me to explain why I was so upset and I eventually shared my fears with them.

At this point, events were to take an unexpected turn. After three more days with Mr and Mrs Brown before returning, they invited me to share their home along with my brother Bill. This took place immediately. Bill had a great interest in cars and took a job as a mechanic at a local garage in Yorkshire and I went to a local school for my final year. It was a very small school but the same problems with literacy affected me there.

Things seemed to go very well living with Mr and Mrs Brown for the first six months. Then Bill decided to move on. He went to sea, joining the Merchant Navy. We were not to meet again for a few years. After a few months of Bill's absence, life became more difficult as I was now the focus of attention and felt inadequate in the face of their expectations. It was not that they were putting a lot of pressure on me but I felt I wasn't delivering the goods with progress in my education. Socially I was doing OK, but I knew this wasn't enough to get me through life in terms of getting work and having a stable income. On finishing my schooling, for a short period of time, I worked in a nursery specialising in trees. This was never enough for me and so, like Bill, I moved on. It was the bright lights for me, returning to my roots in London. It wasn't long before I realised that life had moved on in terms of relationships and that I had changed enormously, both physically and in my life values. I had become very sensitive to people's needs because of my own sufferings in life, yet I was so vulnerable because I didn't know my identity and value as a person.

For a short while I shared accommodation in London with some relatives. During this time, I realised that my life values were different from the values these folk held, but at the same time I recognised they were to be loved and were part of my family. They also loved me, even if this wasn't obvious to me at the time. At this point, I would like to make it known that this story is being written prayerfully so that Jesus will speak through it to those He wants to reach. Even at that time in London, I believe Jesus was teaching me that "love is the greatest" (paraphrase of 1 Corinthians 13:13b). Although I was not able to read at that time, He reached me at my point of need. A personal relationship with Christ wasn't in my life, but the need was there and I did pray every day as calamity after calamity occurred numerous times a day! I recognised a great need for learning and have always been a risk taker, and so I set my heart on seeing as much of this world as I could. Having no money, very few skills but always able to produce the "finished goods", I got by through receiving help and mercy from kind-hearted people. I was allowed to continue my journey through their understanding of my needs. On reflection, God was protecting me all the time as I was to meet many people who were ready to take advantage of me in my vulnerability. Again, I can only recognise this through the Scripture that says, "…therefore be as shrewd as snakes…" (Matthew 10:16). He had yet to teach me to be "…as innocent as doves.", but I had a need for that in my life. It was many years before that need was fulfilled as He knows the time for his purpose within me and I bow before Him in that knowledge. He is never wrong!

Looking back at this time, I feel my heart has always been to help people in need and even at that time, I did feel grateful for the charity that had been shown me. However, with the loss of my family, this was somewhat overshadowed. I can remember being three and a half years old and seeing a homeless couple in London walk onto the bomb ruin near us with two potato sacks. Getting inside the sacks, they cuddled up together and that was their place to sleep that night. It was snowing very lightly at the time. So I'll always be grateful that I had shelter in my childhood and for every night I am blessed with it now. These days, I like to give unconditionally when I see a need, but I am still growing in wisdom about the proportions of giving and sacrifice.

4

The Sea Beckons

London was full of hustle and bustle and I had become used to a quieter life in the North, not forgetting the harsher climate and challenge of walking long distances in the cold to get to school or do shopping. The North had big open spaces where the weather would be unmerciful but we were still expected to be punctual and carry out whatever duties were required each day. In London, I felt protected from the elements but claustrophobic and exposed to a relentless speed of life. After making the decision to try my hand at sea, I thought it would be wise to see if I could cope with this. Being Gordon, I went in at the deep end.

Through help and contacts, I arrived at Lowestoft within weeks of my decision. I spent two or three nights with the Fisherman's Mission, a Christian-based organisation, on the quayside. Three days later, I was on a fishing trawler and heading out into the North Sea. This was my first trip out to sea, and the open space of the ocean made me feel truly free. I thought "how wonderful!", only to discover two or three hours later that the elements at sea became more forceful and my tummy rebelled against this! All the other crew members, about seven in total including the skipper, were fine and found it very amusing. They would delight in getting a rasher of greasy bacon and offering it to me which would make me throw up even more (which I can say was a regular occurrence for the fortnight of the voyage).

Tell It As It Is

The weather deteriorated over the next twenty-four hours into a force nine gale and, being a very small vessel, we were thrown about like a cork, bobbing up and down on the ocean. Worse yet to follow! The day after, the net was cast overboard in the fishing grounds that we had been heading for. More horror! I then learned that they had to be hauled in every few hours, both day and night. We were required to be on deck as the haul was landed. Once landed, the net was emptied of its contents and recast. The fish had to be gutted on the open deck, put into boxes and covered in ice. They were then placed below deck in storerooms. We had about two hours in between each haul in which to sleep, eat and do all other activities! Our main catch was cod and as we progressed we ended up fishing off the coast of Denmark. My sea sickness continued. For their amusement the crew kept offering me cold bacon – this was their entertainment for the voyage! I can remember thinking at the time, "never again will I go to sea!!!"

After about ten days, we started heading back towards England. I can remember a shout going up on deck and everybody pointing. In the distance, I could see the Queen Mary, the huge ocean liner, probably heading somewhere nice. Its movement was nothing like our small trawler bobbing around all over the place. It looked very elegant and graceful and my thoughts were, "that's the kind of vessel I would like to be on!" So on returning to Lowestoft, I left the trawler not waiting to pick my wages up, just so pleased to be back on land. I returned to the bright lights of London without haste.

Although my maiden voyage had been an unpleasant experience, the sea was now in my blood.

The Sea Beckons

Within a matter of months, I joined the Merchant Navy. I was sent to Rotterdam to join my first ship as a "Boy Rating" on deck. Anybody with the role of boy rating would be called "Peggy" by fellow crew members and they were assigned all the menial tasks. This ship was a cargo ship bound for New Orleans to pick up a cargo of grain. It was then to proceed through the Panama Canal, across the Pacific Ocean and on to Japan. It was rather an old ship which would frequently break down. When this happened, many times I prayed that the ship would get back under way as it was very vulnerable in the middle of the Pacific with no engines working. In fact it could quite easily sink if the weather got worse.

To pass the time on a journey, practical jokes were the order of the day. For example, as some of the older crew members would have a drink in the evening and boy ratings were only allowed to drink soft drinks, we would amuse ourselves by taking advantage of the intoxication of the older crew when they got jolly. After they had collapsed in sleep in their cabins we played tricks on them. I would go down to the storeroom, pick up a gallon of syrup off the shelf, gently warm it on the stove to make it runny and gently pour it through the cabin door of one the crew members who'd had a few cans of beer. I would throw the can over the side and return to my cabin to be woken up the next morning with shouts of swearing and cursing and calls of "Who's done this?!" I would come out of my cabin rubbing my eyes and ask, "What's the fuss all about?!", only to see the poor guy trampling around in the syrup which had now thickened to its original form. I had timed this activity carefully, knowing that day was inspection day and soon his cabin would be checked. Of course, I would extend my sympathy to him (love Gordon)!! What fun to be a boy rating! No drink but plenty of activity. It did pass the time of day and was one of many activities to pass long hours at sea.

On Christmas Eve 1963, the ship dropped anchor half a mile out at sea from the mouth of Nagoya harbour. And there in front of us was the majestic sight of Mount Fuji about a mile in the distance with a light covering of snow; an oriental Christmas postcard scene at its best. It was about three in the afternoon, and the crew had been granted shore leave as it was Christmas Eve. We were informed that the liberty boat (lifeboat) would leave the harbour to return to the ship at midnight (this was the only option for returning to the ship that night). I was determined, on leaving the ship, not to have a drink. However, I became mesmerised with the beautiful port of Nagoya and attracted to many of its little bars. I sampled some of the native drinks with the help of my friends. I just managed to return to the port in time to get the boat back to the ship. As I had had a little too much to drink I decided to stand up and sing on the boat. As the boat came alongside the ship the engine was cut and, as I was cut too, I went over the side. I was soon hauled out by a lifeboat hook which ruined my best suit! I promptly went under a hot shower with suit and all just to get warm. Lovely place Japan, good memories, but the bath that evening was rather large and hadn't been that warm – thank goodness for boat hooks!!

On the ship, the first crew member to be called in the morning was "Peggy" who would commence making mugs of tea. These would be taken to the cabins to refresh the fellow crew members who would call the

"Peggy" whatever words were on their lips at the time (not usually complimentary after a heavy night's drinking!). We left Japan having unloaded the cargo and set sail for the port of Callao, in Peru. This port was notorious for crew members getting "rolled" which meant being stripped of all their possessions including clothes, but you would pray that they would leave your underpants on! Within the dock area you were safe but, beyond that, "anything goes". So, sure enough, on one occasion I returned to the ship in my underpants. I hope the clothes fitted the person who took them! What a wonderful life being a boy rating on his first voyage with the minimum of clothes in his suitcase! I was blessed, however, with considerate fellow crew members who soon sorted me out.

Our ship was to take on a cargo of fish meal in sacks and needed stevedores to load the cargo. The cargo was to be kept dry at all times. We headed through the Panama Canal and on to the Bay of Biscay where part of the cargo was deposited and the remainder was taken to the port of Rostock in what was the German Democratic Republic (East Germany). Here, everything I could see from the ship was a delightful grey colour! So the clothes I was wearing were alien to the environment but it was 1963 and the East and West were divided at that time. Even at that time, although I was not a practising Christian, my heart felt strongly for these people. I wanted them to know there was a love in the world which I now appreciate is the great love of God's people. I was now aged eighteen, and I was learning so much of the world – but I had little academic or political understanding of events. I understood the basic needs of man – food, love, care and freedom. I indeed was blessed, although I thought my life was hard at this time. Britain was a free country, with freedom to make mistakes and still receive help. No wonder it was known as "Great" Britain.

On this vessel, we paid off in Rotterdam which means the ship's articles were broken, therefore releasing crew to go home. No flight for us, we did it by train to the Hook of Holland, then by ferry to Harwich and train to London. At this time in my life, I would often return to Phoebe's home and spend about half of my leave with them and the other half would be spent looking around Britain at various beauty spots. If I became lonely during these times, I would wander into a pub for a meal and a few drinks. I would often stand out from the crowd due to having acquired a tan which resulted in me attracting interest and people asking me where I was from. My reply would be, "England!" I would then explain that I was a seaman and this would result in many conversations about where I had been. On returning from a trip to Hawaii, one old gentleman asked me if I carried a box of matches. I looked back at him puzzled and he said, "Well, I believe all the women wear grass skirts." I then understood what he was thinking; I simply smiled and continued drinking my beer!

5

Cruise Liners to Tankers

Sometime in 1964, I made a decision to try my hand on cruise liners and to change from deck crew to catering. I joined a ship which had some eight hundred crew members, mostly men, some of whom were very feminine in nature and theatrical. Being Gordon, I tried to get along with all these people but felt very vulnerable. Often I would tell them little of my own life and when I did, "fairy tales weren't in it." (Meaning it was all fairy tales!)

In my growing wisdom, I learned to decline offers of alcohol. However, I wanted to know how these people ticked. I could appreciate much of what they told me but always had a cut-off point where I could see no purpose or future in their line of thinking. Then I would feel an inner sadness about their situation because I had always longed for a family of my own so my thinking was not the same as theirs. However, many of the people were very pleasant and at this stage of my life, company was company. On meeting the passengers on the liners, I would tell them many stories as we would often pick up passengers from the UK who would alight in the USA and Americans would board who were very inquisitive and loved to engage in conversation. Often they would ask me about my family: let fairy tales commence! I would tell them that my father worked in the local sewage works and that my mother would pick up a pan wherever she could; hence looks of horror! When these passengers had disembarked and new ones came on board, I would tell them my father was an MP and my mother a head teacher of a grammar school. Such a shame they were both dead, it would have brought a smile to their face! Still, it did get me good tips and lots of freebies such as two hundred dollars to spend when I hit port as I had brought much amusement into their life. Often in the evenings our identity would change by putting on a suit and becoming a passenger unbeknown to the officers on the ship. We'd wander up to the bars and order drinks which we would sign for, giving a cabin number. My signature would always be the same, 'M. Mouse' and a fictitious cabin number on a non-existent deck. When they wanted the account settled, they'd realise what the 'M' stood for, "Mickey"! I often took the Mickey.

Through all this, I could not identify who I was regarding my genetic line. Because I had no idea who my father was or my mother, I had no one to imitate and went off on my own understanding of what I thought I should be, which was not always acceptable to people. I really was a rough diamond and learned techniques for survival (i.e. anything goes as long as I wasn't physically injuring people). Let people perceive what they will, as far as I was concerned, I needed food, shelter and love. I longed for a stable relationship in my life but had never met anyone who could affect me deeply. I waited another three years before this happened.

I then changed to tankers which required much safety knowledge and endurance. Frequently calling at many of the Persian Gulf ports, we would often bring the crude oil to the UK or the Continent for refining. This was the Sixties, many people were buying cars for the first time and UK industry was taking off. The country was definitely on fire regarding ambition in commerce, but I wasn't carrying a box of matches! My own thinking was, "anything is possible if you can play the part." This is the point when I was given advice by my contemporaries, mainly older people who said, "Listen to me son, bull**** baffles brains." Not the best piece of advice (it's not true), but one I practiced for many years. How could someone who was illiterate and had no parents to support him find his way in life? I really could have done with a role model but always gave my best in my work and tried to avoid fiddles. When I could see there was a moral conflict in work activities I would withdraw without giving an explanation to anyone as I had not learned how to confront people on issues that mattered to me.

Slowly, as the years went by, I was gaining promotions and taking responsibility for duties to be carried out on board and had to be quite firm at times when crew members started getting lazy. As I joined a ship, I would often make a point of demonstrating diligence in my work so that others could observe in the hope that they would carry out their duties in the same way. A small amount of negligence in issues of hygiene could result in loss of life of crew members as there were no doctors on-board due to the low numbers of crew – it wasn't a marine statutory requirement. My attitude of taking care in my work stuck with me and later in life, people would say, "You expect to have all your t's crossed and i's dotted." Today I believe that if you are faithful in little things, you'll be faithful in big things as is expressed in the Bible (Matthew 25:21). However little or big a task is, we should let our "Yes" be yes and our "No" mean no (Matthew 5:37). I believe that we should do things to the best of our ability and not feel ashamed of what others think about what we are doing as long as our heart is pure.

6

Adventure Down Under

& in the Middle East

We were often taken to places like Australia to supply crude oil in sparsely populated areas but there was always someone to make a living off the backs of crew members from various ships. On one trip, I remember going ashore, and walking through a refinery. Just outside the gates was a battered old caravan with a vendor selling delicious meat pies. Being young and always hungry I purchased one, only to find that a matter of hours later I had a bad tummy ache and all that goes with it, until it passed through my system. Coming across this same caravan thirty-six hours later I shouted to the man, "What was in those pies?" He replied with a smile, "Kangaroo." My reply was, "Up you too!" to which he replied, "You pommy bast****. Bleep, bleep, bleep!" Such was remote Australia at that time; everyone has to make a living! I certainly wasn't in a comfort zone regarding that pie, but later I discovered that true life is not about being in a comfort zone but about embracing the challenges of life for the better.

On leaving Australia we returned to the Persian Gulf. We loaded a new cargo of crude oil and returned to the UK via the Suez Canal. We were the last convoy to pass through the canal by a matter of hours before the Six Day Arab-Israeli War (1967) commenced which affected safe passage through the canal. On returning to the UK, the refinery we came into was the Isle of Grain on the Thames estuary. We broke articles and said our goodbyes and went our separate ways. Each one of us had to learn to accept that although we had spent several months together we were not close friends but colleagues who would then have to move on to a different vessel.

Then, reality would set in in my life once more – lots of money in my pocket, but where was I going to spend my time on leave? Sometimes I would pop by and say hello to Phoebe but she had four children of her own and it would have been difficult for her to accommodate me. So I spent time in hotels where I had some horrific experiences.

For example, when I was feeling lonely, I would wander down to the bar and have a drink. I would usually get involved in conversation and often there would be the question, "What do you do for a living?", and I would let them know I was a seaman. But many times it would result in difficulty. Often, the person I was talking to would want me to come back to his hotel room and have a drink with him and I would find that everything was not innocent and I would make a run for it! I lost more and more self-esteem through situations like that in my life and I felt very alone in the world with no protection of family. I felt that I was wanted as a commodity and that was the only way people viewed me rather than people seeing me as Gordon. I was quite naive in my relationships with people. These days, I have to really know people, not by what they say but by what they are before I establish close friendship (as Christ says, "By their fruit you will recognise them..." Matthew 7:16a). Having said this, I recognise that

Christians are saved by grace, not by any value they have in themselves. This understanding is one of the biggest blessings in my life which I received at the age of fifty-eight, a long time ahead.

When my leave time finished, I joined my next vessel. In my heart, there was a sigh of relief because I felt comfortable and had a purpose and value as a seaman. At this time, I returned to the Persian Gulf to bring crude oil back into Europe.

On one occasion, I was in the Port of Kharg Island in Iran when we were informed that the Shah of Persia was to visit the port. We were given instructions on how to conduct ourselves and had a very firm warning of the dangers of not following instructions. The reason for this was that the Shah was surrounded by guards with automatic weapons and we had been instructed not to put our hands in our pockets as this could have endangered our lives. We had been running around to make the ship look presentable including painting one side of the ship that the Shah would see but the other side we were very pleased he wouldn't see as in no way did we want to insult him! The temperatures in the Persian Gulf were usually one hundred and twenty degrees Celsius, so we would often change clothes four times a day and spend our evenings doing "dhobi," which is a seaman's term for washing clothes or linen. Our recreation included playing table tennis. However, when I tried it on land it was not quite the same, as no rolling was involved; in fact and I have never mastered the game on terra firma to this day!

On returning from the Persian Gulf, if we had a light enough cargo we would return via the Red Sea and call in at the port of Aden. At this time, our troops were stationed in Aden and it was a very volatile situation. Against advice, we would often visit Steamer Point in Aden where alcohol was available and we would join with the armed forces in that area. But we were always aware of the danger. For example, sometimes a sewer drain cover would open, and we would be sent a nice present, namely a hand grenade. Dangerous stuff indeed, all for the sake of a drink! I really had what I now appreciate as "footprints in the sand" taking place in my life. ("Footprints in the Sand" is the title of a popular allegorical poem of disputed authorship which communicates the faithfulness of God in our lives through difficult circumstances.) As we left Aden, we would proceed up the Red Sea and through the Suez Canal, west across the Mediterranean and around to the Bay of Biscay. Crossing the Bay of Biscay could often be quite rough as tankers had no stabilisers. We proceeded up to the English Channel to come into a UK refinery.

Just for a break from routine, sometimes I would be placed on a smaller vessel to take refined fuel, often from Gothenburg, to ports in the UK, mostly in more versatile tankers. I would not have appreciated a balloon being popped on these vessels, might set off the wrong idea! Gothenburg is a beautiful area and, on one occasion, I ventured ashore and visited Stockholm. SHOCK! Scandinavia was much more liberal in its approach to sexual matters, as demonstrated in the poster advertisements on display. For me though, at this time, it was a big shock and a fear. Within myself, I knew it wasn't right that people's bodies should be exposed in this way, yet in this part of the world it was being considered as freedom. I felt as a person, my values were being violated and many questions were to arise in my heart from this visit. Along with my other experiences of violence in different places I was trying to work out my values and becoming more confused. If only I could have had the opportunity to talk these things through with parents. There was no safety net for me to grow at this point in my life in sound understanding, yet I would still pray. Who was I praying to? I knew it was this man called "God" who I'd met very early in life when I stole the flowers from the altar in the church.

7

Love at First Sight

On one occasion in 1967, I paid off in the Isle of Grain and travelled to London. My eldest brother had married, so I paid him a visit on this leave. I was informed that the wife of one of my half-brothers was in hospital and I thought it would be a nice gesture to take her some flowers. Through this simple act, my life was to change forever because I was to meet June who I married two years later. I can clearly remember that June was sitting one side of the hospital bed and I was on the other. So when I tell people that I met my wife over a bed I can have a clear conscience and tongue in cheek! But in all seriousness, I can say that I found June very attractive and she made an impression on me that I have never forgotten.

On leaving the hospital, June was walking ahead of me down the corridor towards the exit when a friend of June's whispered to me, "She's single!" Although I was very nervous, in an act of bravery, I walked up to June and asked her if she would like to come for a drink. The response was, "No, I'm a Methodist." Being Gordon, my response was, "What, a meths drinker?" To add insult to injury I asked her out for the following evening. June's response was, "I'm washing my hair." Having summoned up all this courage, I wasn't going to give up easily and continued asking her out. I think June, in desperation, agreed to a date and we met later that week. Many years later I found out that June had gone home and told her mum that she'd met a lovely man named Gordon.

June, having given me her address, asked me to meet her at her home. Unfortunately on this evening, there was the most awful thunderstorm, but being a seaman, I would turn up on time no matter what the weather. However, having just returned from the Pacific, I had no coat. On arriving at June's door, I heard her mum saying to her, "No man would turn up on a night like this in their right mind!" My response was to knock on the door louder than usual which June's mother opened quickly and I stood before her like a drowned rat. Then my eyes gazed beyond her mum and I realised I was early and June was in her full glory, rollers and all in her hair. I thought, "Great stuff Gordon, you've messed this one up too!", but better things were to happen later!

June's mum immediately invited me downstairs into their basement living room. There I met June's two younger sisters and her father and June was to follow down shortly afterwards looking quite radiant, no sign of a curler! Her mother pulled the settee around the electric fire. Having given me a towel to dry my hair and with steam coming off my clothes, she asked me to take my shoes off so she could dry them. They really were wet as they were suede and, being winkle-pickers, they had pointed toes. I witnessed her putting them onto two prongs in front of the fire. I really was quite nervous of meeting June's family for the first time on this, our first date. I was sitting on the settee with June and her two younger sisters were sitting on dining room chairs behind us. I was shocked to hear one whispering to another, "He's got a clean neck!" My thoughts were,

Love at First Sight

"Bloody cheek!" At the same time, I was witnessing the demise of my lovely suede shoes, my one and only pair. The toes were curling up and steam was rising from them but I was too nervous to say a word. All I can say about this was, if you've seen the shoes Aladdin wears with beautiful curled up toes, mine were in the process of taking up this appearance (smile Gordon – you've got a date!). At about eleven o'clock, having been left alone in the front room for an hour, June's mum was to call out from the kitchen, "It's getting late June. You have work in the morning." Understanding what her mum meant, I said to June, "I think I'd better be going." We said our goodbyes in the passage way where June put her arms around me. I sensed from June that she was expecting nothing in return for her affection and I was completely baffled by this. I had never experienced such a lovely act of kindness. I didn't know how to respond to June's love. "Love" was a word I knew but I didn't understand it. I think this was my first encounter of a deep unconditional love.

From this point on my life went into turmoil where I went into denial, but June wasn't one for giving up. She was suddenly to appear in my life unexpectedly, twenty-four hours before I joined my next ship. This made things even harder in my life as I promised to write to her and she had left me her address. Whoops! I could barely read and definitely couldn't write. Spelling was a non-starter, yet I wanted to know her more and felt she would never want to know someone with such lack of skills. What a dilemma! But God is a good God. On joining my next ship, I could never get the thought of June out of my mind. It really was a voyage of wonder, tears and despair. How was I going to keep in contact? I received a letter from June, making things even more difficult. She would expect a reply! June received my reply at the next port. After being sneaky with other crew, asking them, "How do you spell so and so?" at various intervals, I would use the excuse that my mind had gone blank. This was quite true as there was nothing in there regarding spelling! I know June was to get one or two lines at the maximum as a reply. But the most powerful thing I was able to write was, "I think I am in love with you." In all that simplicity and transparency, our relationship started to grow on both sides. It was my birthday on this voyage and a bigger thing was to happen. I can remember for years and this will never leave me, on returning to the UK, I received a big parcel and many birthday cards from June and her family. I can remember sitting in my cabin, unable to open anything and thinking, "Can this be for me?" I could not stop my tears and I'll never feel ashamed of saying so. About thirty minutes later, I was able to open them. That was just the start of a new chapter in my life and the things that lay ahead.

I spent my leave with my elder brother in his new home with his wife in rather cramped conditions, but it was a roof over my head. And I was able to spend time with June and her family. We would often go for walks each evening, along the Embankment and through St James's Park. On Sundays, June's mum would pack a picnic for both of us and we would spend the day in Richmond. Life really was wonderful, a new experience for me. At the end of my leave, I couldn't bear to think of returning to sea. I was thinking up every way possible to be able to stay with June. The best thing I could come up with was to say that I had haemorrhoids due to the heat in the Persian Gulf. It was true, but I did play on it! Ringing up the marine personnel, I requested permission to be released on medical grounds. The reply being, "What's wrong with you?" My reply was, "I've got haemorrhoids." Their reply was, "No trouble, we can have you in hospital by next week and all will be taken care of." At this point, I began to stutter. I think the person on the end of the phone who I'd known for years felt sorry for me and said, "Have you met someone Gordon?" This man knew of my history and told me that I was immediately released. I had quite a period of time in service to fulfil but he let me go. As I was to find out, I was paid for the period of time that I had remaining and all my National Insurance (stamp) contributions were covered. What a blessing. Greater things were to happen the next day.

8

Tea & Coffee

I walked into a tea and coffee shop to buy some Darjeeling tea. They used to roast their coffee on the premises and many different types of tea were on the shelves. As I stood at the counter, the person serving me said, "You look a nice, clean young man. You're not looking for a job are you?" My response was, "Yes, I've just left sea." Unbeknown to me, I was speaking with the owner of the company which imported tea and coffee and had retail shops in the West End and one on the South Coast. God really is a good God. I arrived the following week with my documents of sea service and a baffled look on the gentleman's face. How was a man getting wages and stamps paid way in advance? All I could say to the man was, "Ring this number", which he did, in another office. He returned with a smile on his face, although still scratching his head. "When can you start?" he asked me. I think I started the following week.

I fitted into the job with ease and was able to roast coffee and serve customers and get a real rapport with people. The shop seemed to be filling up all the time but my mind was working overtime. As questions were asked, great stories were to be told. I wanted that sale! Example: There were lots of drawers of coffee behind the counter and many of the customers that visited the shop were office workers who enjoyed fresh coffee. They would buy the coffee beans to take home and grind themselves. I would give the impression that I understood about coffee but really I understood nothing. I would go back to a barrow-boy mentally (which was market-stall salesmanship). I would put my hand into the draw of coffee and explain to them that the coffee in my hand was of a fairly large bean and grown at a certain altitude. This would result in them having a look of understanding on their face. I would put my hand back into the same draw and return it back to the counter saying to them, "As you can see, this one is of an entirely different bean and grown at a much lower altitude." So, on my recommendation, I would advise them to buy the dearer bean, which was the same as the cheaper bean and everyone would be happy and grateful. We made a good profit and that was my idea of business – no one complained! I was often referred to as "Honest Gov." by people who knew me more intimately.

During the time I worked in the coffee shop, I continued to court June – but I came to realise I had a rival. This rival being a little pet poodle named Sparky. Unfortunately, Sparky was quite blind and refused to sit anywhere but next to June so I would often sit on the floor, resting my head on June's leg, ignoring Sparky. One time, forgetting he was blind, I moved my head quite fast, startling Sparky. His response was to sink his teeth into my head to protect June. I think it was the first time June heard me swear. Bleep, bleep, bleep – with roars of laughter all around. That dog had to go! As I explained to June, he couldn't see objects and was often bumping into them. One of the reasons I loved June was her heart for animals, especially animals that are suffering. She couldn't face having Sparky put down but truthfully, I could only see him suffering as he was constantly frightened. I don't really think he saw me as a rival but I was just not used to him and his needs. About six months later, Sparky was put down. This was quite upsetting at the time.

My work in the coffee shop sometimes involved providing holiday cover in another shop near St Martin's Lane. My customers at this shop would often be men from the royal ballet who would call me "Darling". I wasn't too pleased at this and explained to them that I'd left my darling at home that morning, still asleep in bed. This would result in them leaving the shop with a blank look on their face and asking when the usual shop manager would be back at which point I would shout, "Two weeks' time!" One day I had an accident with a coffee roaster; it exploded, burning away part of my hair. My assistant, a lady of fifty-five, ran outside the shop. I was quickly on her heels and she said, "Now look what you've done!" I wasn't aware of how I looked at that time. But on the arrival of the shop owners, there was both concern and laughter. Everything was intact in the shop – the only things missing were my eyebrows, my eyelashes and my fringe. I was taken to the Royal Eye Hospital as my eyes felt like they were full of grit, but all was well. Lots of cream was pumped into them and I had the rest of the day off. I was quite nervous of roasting machines after that, but I continued nevertheless. I think the shop assistant left shortly after!

After I'd run the coffee shop for about eighteen months to two years, June and I were to get married. It really was a great occasion. We were married in a little church in Kennington Lane, Lambeth, South East London. There were lots of family members present. I think more of June's family than mine, as I had got two full brothers and only half relatives after that. This took place in June 1969. I think it was the hottest day of the year but it wouldn't have mattered if it was the coldest. I think June will never forget this day, and neither will I. As I waited at the bottom of the aisle for June to come down, I was overcome with how beautiful she looked. Meeting her at the altar and being so nervous, I said to her, "Cor blimey!" I'll never know what made that come out, it really was pure nerves and something had to come out, why that, I'll never know. I think I goofed! But all was forgiven, we were getting married. It really was the happiest day of my life. A treasure I hold in my heart to this day. We spent our honeymoon in Cornwall which commenced the next day. We stayed in Bude and had a house on the cliff top overlooking Bude bay. It wasn't very commercialised at this time. We had a very happy fortnight there.

We returned to London where we had secured a flat. It had just one bedroom, a kitchen, bathroom and living room. It was our first home and we both felt very happy and I knew I was very fulfilled. We were unsure as to where we were going to spend the rest of our lives, we thought possibly Australia. But all I could think about was kangaroo pies – no thank you! So we continued in London for about two or three years. In September 1971, our first daughter was born and we realised our flat was too small. In the previous year, June and I had saved very hard with the hope of purchasing a property on the outskirts of London. We managed to accumulate enough money to pay half the value of a reasonable property but house prices were rising at five hundred pounds a month and gazumping was taking place. Even when we first started looking, the average house price was already two thousand pounds, a huge amount at that time. It began to look as if our hopes of getting our own place in or near London would be dashed. So we started looking at other options – including the possibility of living in one of the new towns.

9

Relocation

Eventually we settled for a new town in Suffolk and moved there in May 1972. On arriving in our new house, and ready to start a new job which was in the food industry as a butcher, I was informed not to turn up for work. Our first daughter had contracted salmonella before leaving London and the company was very nervous of contamination entering their factory. They asked me to stay at home for two months on full pay. Suited me fine! Much to do in a new house, but then suggestions started coming that maybe it would be wise to look for other employment. I think I had become an unnecessary expense.

At this point in my life, I tried my hand at engineering with much disaster to follow. I got a job with a company that provided industrial refrigeration products. I went through the usual procedure of an interview, where I was informed that I was very suitable. I was put into one of the manufacturing sections where it was necessary to read technical drawings, both of English projection and an American method known as Third Angle, which required a different way of looking at things. Unfortunately, I had never looked at a technical drawing before in my life, but being Gordon, I kept quiet. I wanted the job! I don't think it took the older people in that section more than an hour to start having a good laugh, but I wasn't worried, it was a job. They were very good to me as older men and explained, with great patience, how to interpret technical drawings to find the correct angles for drilling. However, I found the two different drawing methods to be confusing and spent the next six months producing rubbish. The bins were always full with plenty added by me!

Towards the end of those six months, the factory employees were called to a meeting which was about the company offering a new pension scheme. I listened with great interest as all the senior staff were there offering this great opportunity which came before the government had had the opportunity to put their saving scheme forward. At the end of the meeting which lasted about an hour, we were asked, "Are there any questions?" I noticed that no one stood up, but Gordon did. My question was, "If you are offering your scheme to us without us knowing what the government will offer, it's not very democratic and I believe we live in a democracy?" Red faces were all around. The meeting closed shortly afterwards. I was approached by the management the next day and asked where I was educated. Looking at them directly in the face, and being very sarcastic, I said, "At one of the finest institutions in the country." They said, "Where's that?", whereupon I said, "Borstal" (this being the name of a reform school of the time for delinquent young people). This was not true but I felt that as they had shown contempt for my intelligence I would do likewise to them. Not the wisest way to resolve the situation! However, the wages were very low at this company and I was no person cut out for light engineering work, so I left the job.

Life continued and I fancied the open air and became a milkman. My new home town really was a place where you could try your hand at anything. I went along to the local dairy and was met with much interest by the foreman. After talking with him for fifteen minutes, I was offered a job. Oh dear! In those days, the milk floats were all petrol engined which made them very noisy. I used to get up at three in the morning, go down to the dairy yard, load up my milk and start my round at four o'clock. The street lights would not be switched on until around five so I was in complete darkness. I became a master at holding a torch in my mouth and two crates of milk, one in each hand. I would hear moans from the upper windows of houses as I drew up outside customers' homes as the engine rumbled in the background. On top of this, there would be the rattle of milk bottles, particularly the empty ones going back into crates. I loved the job nonetheless. I met many people when I collected the money on a Friday and, over a period of time, they got to know me very well. One old lady used to insist, when it was very cold, that I come inside her home at five in the morning and have a glass of her home-made wine which happened to be very strong. So when I returned to the float, things became even noisier with me colliding with curbs. Other customers further along my round would offer me additional beverages, but I would try to show restraint, not wanting to make my journey more hazardous.

Unfortunately this job was becoming quite difficult. On one particular part of my round, the customers did not want to pay for their milk and I had to carry a huge debit list forward each week. This list continued to grow and it became time consuming to sort out. I was commissioned on the sale of milk in addition to receiving a basic wage. I don't think I received one penny on increasing the sales of milk. I was working long hours, seventy a week on average. The deciding factor for me to leave this job came at Christmas, when large orders were placed for fresh cream and yoghurt. Having fully loaded my float, I parked up to deliver to a customer, only to return to the float to find all the yoghurt and cream had disappeared! I think I just about broke even that Christmas, having received many tips from customers. It was time to quit. Great time Christmas Eve! There was no float to unload that day – they helped themselves and I had no way of recouping the money as I had no idea who had done it. I was greeted on Boxing Day morning by knocking on our door. The foreman was there from the dairy. "You're late for work," he stated. I replied, "What work? I'm quitting because the milk keeps disappearing. I can't make any money out of the job." Happy days, but I have always been a trier and didn't understand my journey at this point in my life.

10

Evolution or Creation?

In 1973, June became pregnant with our second daughter. During June's pregnancy, there was a knock on the door. As I opened it, I was confronted with the question, "Do you believe in evolution or creation?" I replied, "Creation." As I thought about what I had said, there was some confusion within my heart. I had found true love in my relationship with June but, outside of that, I couldn't see God's love in the midst of my painful upbringing. I could appreciate that His creation is beautiful in itself, but people in the creation had let me down.

These people seemed friendly, so I continued chatting with them. They introduced themselves as Jehovah's Witnesses (JWs). Before I met June, my elder brother had had a doorstep encounter with JWs, so the name "Jehovah" was familiar to me and he told me it was God's name. He'd also told me one of their beliefs about how Jesus died, claiming that He was killed on a stake. So being none the wiser, and trying to be amiable, I told these JWs that the church had got it wrong and that Jesus had died on a stake. Because I had been forced to sit through church services when desperate to go to the toilet and wasn't allowed to move or fidget, I was prejudiced against the church. I saw it as a place of strict authoritarian rule and I considered faith to be irrelevant to my life. I wanted an alternative viewpoint on things I knew to be true and so I developed a relationship with these people. As we met together on various occasions, they began to point out faults within the church. This fitted in with my thinking at that time because church had been forced upon me and I disliked the way I was treated there. Because of my lack of reading ability, I would sit and listen to the JWs' teaching and simply absorb what I was being told without questioning things for myself. After six months, I was baptised as a Jehovah's Witness. Despite this, there was still a lack of understanding of what true love was apart from the love June had showed me. It was only after I came to Christ that I could truly understand the greatest love which Christ showed in dying for us.

June was very unhappy with our involvement with the JWs. However, she had always had a Christian belief and was confirmed in the Church of England at the age of eleven. She chose to get baptised with the JWs but her motivation was to serve God rather than join the JWs' organisation. In being baptised, June felt a connection with God and that the Holy Spirit was present. June knew that within the JWs' beliefs, to have a blood transfusion was not acceptable. With the imminent arrival of our second daughter, this must have been a heavy burden for June to carry. I was totally insensitive towards June about this; I had become very indoctrinated with the JWs' teachings. The people were appealing and the friendships I was forming were good but there was nothing spiritual happening within me; I was the same old Gordon inside with the same difficulties. Going forward as a person was just not happening. I wasn't able to talk about real things that were happening in my life and the deeper sadness inside.

Evolution or Creation?

When the time came for June's delivery of our second daughter, it was February 1974, snowing and pitch dark outside. In the early hours of the morning, I went across the road to call an ambulance from the phone box. To my horror, they answered me by telling me I'd have to wait. I then decided to call the police, dialling 999, to inform them that I didn't know how to deliver a baby. I told them the ambulance people said I would have to wait and that June's contractions were happening every two to three minutes. The reply from the police was, "We'll see about that." To my great relief, an ambulance arrived within four minutes. My daughter and I waved goodbye to June and returned to the comfort of the house with her clinging tightly to me for the remainder of the night. June's delivery was complicated by a haemorrhage and blood clots. However, by the grace of God, June got through the birth without a blood transfusion.

On reflection, the joy of having our second child together was diminished by fear of the possibility of needing a blood transfusion and going against the JWs' teaching. I couldn't connect love with this teaching, it seemed brutal. The whole experience had been detrimental to our marriage relationship. I was searching for a loving God who did more than give us rules, but I still didn't understand what true love was outside of my marriage.

During our time as JWs, we had involvement with Christians, one of whom was a friend of June from London who had worked with her as a civil servant. He was very concerned for both of us and came to our town on various occasions. He encouraged us to mix with local Christians who could support us in our journey. So we had JWs seeking to draw us into their community and Christians doing likewise. I had been put off church by my early experiences but I knew God existed so I would give anything a go that promised a relationship with Him. During one of my low points I went into the local parish church and got on my knees before God and was seeking His guidance. All I can say about that is that I had a sense of calmness and, on leaving the church building, I decided to share this experience with the JW leaders. I was asked in a gentle way whether I felt sorry that I had done this. I could only say no as I had really experienced comfort in that time of prayer. I was then called before the leaders and asked to repent of this act. But again I refused because it felt right and good. I eventually parted company with the JWs although it did feel painful to leave them at the time.

11

Breakdown

In the period leading up to my major breakdown, I had a variety of jobs. One of these was with a company that relocated to Scotland which I decided not to move with. I also worked for a removal company which was a learning experience for me. I didn't really appreciate the relative value of household items.

Early on in the job, I and another young man, who was equally as ignorant, were sent to a large house to relocate a farmer to a much smaller retirement house. We were asked to remove his wardrobe which seemed very old and heavy. The first thing I noticed was that it had lots of pin-sized holes in it and so I considered it as rubbish. As we tried to move it, we were put off because of the weight and quick thinking led to an alternative option. We grabbed a mattress from a bed, placed it in the hall and passed the wardrobe over the banister. Tongue in cheek, I was pre-empting the days of health and safety; we didn't want to hurt our backs! Unfortunately, using this method caused the departure of the doors from the main body of the wardrobe. Quick thinking once more resulted in the reattachment of the doors and nothing mentioned to others. Maybe at a later date it was realised that the doors weren't quite right. Everybody's got to make a living, Gordon included! Another job I had was moving a couple from an upstairs flat in one of the villages. They had a large chest freezer which was fully loaded with ice. Unfortunately, when we came to move it, it made a quicker descent down the stairs than planned and acquired a dent along the way. Once more, nothing was said. It was carefully placed in its new home with the dented side out of sight. Oh dear, I'd had no training for the job. Eventually the job became too physically demanding and I left.

Around 1976, I had some good news regarding the trainee butcher vacancy which I had initially applied for after moving to Suffolk. Because my first daughter was clear of salmonella, I was able to reapply for the job. I started immediately as a trainee. The average training period for this job was four to six weeks to ensure you could work at an acceptable speed. I can truthfully say I never attained the expected speed in the time I was there. The meat was coming to me on a conveyer belt and because I was not able to process it quick enough, I had to pile it up at the side and occasionally it would finish up on the floor or on me.

The hardest thing for me at the factory was the tremendous noise that we were subjected to. After a period of just a couple of months, it started to affect my health although I refused to acknowledge this. I am a man that needs a degree of quietness and I had never worked in a factory environment before coming to Suffolk. I can remember, one morning, setting off for work in my car and as I got to the top of a hill I stopped in the road. All I remember after this was many people knocking on the car windows with great anger asking me what I was doing. I felt unable to answer or move or alter the situation. But someone who recognised me asked me to get into the passenger seat and he drove me home. On coming through the front door, I burst into tears. June was very calm and asked me to go to the doctor. I felt very weak physically and just remember arriving at the doctors. On entering his room, the tears flowed. He sat me down and explained that he believed I was having a breakdown. This was to hit me so hard for it seemed at that moment that my dreams had come to an end. I had been blessed with two lovely daughters, a beautiful wife and a home. All I wanted to do at that time was to provide for my family and give them a good home. I was unable to accept that I was having a breakdown and, on returning home, I laid on the settee and June asked me what the doctor had said. I told June that my heart was a bit weak. I just felt such stigma and failure in my life. The only thing I had to offer was my physical strength, to be able to work hard, but it was quite obvious to me that this had gone and I needed help big time. I was given some tablets to take and they had a very calming effect on me and it felt a pleasant place to be at that time.

It was agreed that I should go to the main city nearby to see a top psychiatrist where I would have the opportunity to discuss my situation. As it was no longer safe for me to drive, I travelled by bus to keep my appointment which was six weeks later. I can remember on this particular day it was pouring with rain. It was quite a walk from getting off the bus to where I was to have this meeting. I was on time and within ten minutes of arriving I was greeted by a consultant psychiatrist. I had been told that I would have about two hours with the consultant before returning home. On shaking his hand on my arrival he said, "I'm afraid I'm running late. I've only got four minutes to talk with you." My heart sank deeply as I thought that any form of help wasn't going to be given me. I replied to him with a rude comment as I felt that I was being overlooked and my self-esteem hit rock bottom. The appointment ended abruptly in less than four minutes. On returning home, a few days later I revisited my GP and explained what had taken place. All I can remember was my GP saying, "I'm so sorry, I'm so very sorry. All I can do is offer you these tablets." And that was to be my journey for the next twenty-seven years and it was to be a downward journey.

When I think back on these times, my heart still feels very sad. I was unable to tell anybody what was troubling me as the psychotic medication made my thoughts very vivid and I was on several different medications at the same time. Although I was not aware of my behaviour (it seemed quite normal to me), I can appreciate now that I was acting bizarrely. June and my children must have been very embarrassed at times but, at the time, it was just normal life to me. I still had that inability to relax and let go, believing that I was unable to achieve anything of value. They really were dark times. June would tell me that I would stare at people. I was not aware of this at all. I used to tell people that I was on drugs and now realising that this was often interpreted that I was on street drugs.

Regarding time, I lost concept of days and weeks and even the rhythm of day and night. I couldn't see anything in proper perspective. Reality had become unreal to the point where I didn't properly recognise my own body and its functioning or movement. In terms of speech or thinking, I had no inhibitions. For example, I was in a church meeting one day with friends and I stood up and now can remember singing, "You will get no beer up in heaven, I don't want to go there." I think my friends were very understanding, but all I could think about was that these people weren't like me. However, I couldn't change and all I could be to others was me, lost in this world of psychotic medication. I wasn't aware of it at the time but people were very tolerant of me and very loving towards me. I think bits of my history came out to those around me throughout various times in my illness but I always blamed myself for my condition. I had had many opportunities as a young man but some of these I was unable to take advantage of. I now understand the reason why, but at the time, I simply blamed myself just as others who knew me had blamed me.

12

Temple Scan

As my illness progressed, it was agreed that I should be admitted to a mental hospital. This happened in 1976. I felt enormous insecurity about this as it was an institution and I had spent my childhood in institutions. I felt very fearful. This was to be the pattern of my life for the next twenty years – time at home followed by time in mental institutions. In the early years of being admitted, I had several brain scans. In one of my clearer times, it had been explained that they believed I'd received damage on my temple through a forceps delivery at birth and that had severely impacted my ability to learn literacy skills. I was told that a connection in the brain on the temple was acting as a sparking plug instead of a direct line. My own understanding of this is that my ability in literacy, in particularly spelling, is very limited. But I can compensate in my vocabulary and in my ability to remember things I have learned.

It is easy for me to recognise people who have these same situations in their lives but I would never want to confront anyone. I have great admiration for those who look to overcome literacy problems or any other difficulties in life. The encouraging thing for me is that in our weakness is our strength. To write this testimony, I have had to make a decision to put the effort in, working with a brother, to express what God has done for me. I think of Moses and his weakness in speaking and God's provision for him in carrying out his ministry to confront Pharaoh. Although Moses believed he was unable to be used as God's spokesperson to Pharaoh, he was given Aaron, a fluent speaker, to accomplish God's purpose.

Although I was ill, I longed to work. Before and after my breakdown, there would be a pattern of better times through the summer months followed by depression in the winter. Early on in my illness, my condition eased a little and some time in or around 1977, I managed to get clearance from my doctor to go back to work. I still had my driving licence at this time and felt quite confident in my driving. I managed to obtain a job with the Home Office as a driver. My job involved driving lorries of various kinds, minibuses and other vehicles. Often it would be to visit prisons all over the country and occasionally to bring supplies to other government establishments. I would often go to central London on the job. The job gave me a sense of identity and worth and the satisfaction of being able to fulfil my role as a husband and father.

But, in all truthfulness, I was feeling stressed and I was doing less and less driving in the job and working more and more with prison inmates. I used to act as a supervisor over a group of inmates as they carried out their daily tasks. I can remember asking prisoners how they were coping with life in prison and whether they felt sorry that they were in prison. In most cases, the reply was, "I'm sorry I got caught." This sank my heart and to this day, I struggle to accept that kind of attitude. These days, one of my prayers is that God would move in a mighty way within the hearts of prison inmates. My wife often reminds me that everybody was once an innocent baby and their life experience has brought them to where they are. Everybody needs healing. I believe that there is a great cry in people's hearts for a way forward in their life, both within family relationships and release from their torment. And I know that the cross that Jesus suffered and died on was for that very purpose. That each man can leave all his shame and all his pain right there and live because He rose again.

In my job with the Home Office I was having periods when I was admitted to hospital and my employers were very understanding. There were always offers of help in many ways. I was helped financially with a number of benefits to cover for my mental illness. But within myself I was struggling with receiving this free help as, from my time in care, I had been taught that I should pay my way in life. I wanted to give my best in all things I did. I felt inferior; I didn't want to be dependent on handouts and wanted the satisfaction of achieving things for myself. Since my first breakdown, nothing had truly been resolved. I'd been taking medication to cover the problem, but once again I was feeling hopeless and more despondent about my failure to cope. I knew of no one in the town I lived in that had a similar background to mine, being brought up in care having lost both parents. I felt I couldn't fit in with others who had enjoyed the privileged background of having loving parents and family.

I went back into a psychiatric hospital and was told I could go back to work even if it was just for one day a week for an indefinite time. But I couldn't cope with those terms. I still felt I had to work for my money. I got to the stage where there was no reality in my life and no purpose. I felt a failure. As I was in no fit state to work, I left the Home Office at the end of 1982. My condition continued the same for many years after this.

Around 1989, I began attending a local church in my home town. As I mentioned earlier, the medication I was taking left me free of inhibitions and so my behaviour was strange but, nonetheless, I found acceptance in this church. They supported me through really difficult times and were always willing to pray with me. But my dependence was on people, not on God, and so it was to people I would turn for answers. This pattern of people dependence continued for about fourteenth years.

13

BREAKTHROUGH

One morning in 2003, I came down for breakfast and for some unknown reason to me, my hand hit the table and I shouted, "I cannot live my life without Jesus in it!" I was aware that this had frightened June, but I told her that I was alright. She told me she was leaving for work but I could see the fear in her eyes of what had just taken place.

We said our goodbyes, but I instinctively knew that she would go to the doctors and mention what had just taken place. I went to our bedroom, got on my knees and cried out to God in distress. I told Him I was sorry that I had not let Him in all my life and I needed Him now more than ever before. I cried a lot and just lay on the bed, exhausted. But a great calming effect came upon me and I really felt His presence inside of me. Although I never heard a physical voice, I knew He was inside me and sensed that everything would be alright. I was waiting for the phone to ring and seemingly on cue, it rang. I was requested to come to the doctor's surgery as soon as possible.

So I got dressed and arrived about three quarters of an hour later. I was immediately sent in to see the doctor. June was sitting there as I entered his room and I duly said to the doctor, "Good morning, are you well?" The doctor replied, "I've never seen you so calm Gordon." He looked at June and said, "There's no need for him to be admitted to hospital." I think June was confused, but I had met my Heavenly Father in a mighty way. My journey has been eventful with many highs and lows but this was an almighty high. After this I took no more psychotic medication. This was against everyone's advice – but God had taken over.

I was told by the doctors I could die. My weight went from around eighteen stone to roughly ten in a matter of six or seven weeks. I can remember the doctor saying, "You need testing for diabetes." I said, "I've no need to be tested for that," but he insisted as no-one can lose weight in this way without some explanation. I was never diagnosed with diabetes. However, the weight loss was, in part, caused by my loss of appetite during the six or seven week time period after my breakthrough. I was making a tremendous number of cakes for the church I was part of but everyone was advising me to rest. My viewpoint was that I was so glad to be alive and thinking clearly, and I wanted to contribute and be a part of my community once again. That very much included the church.

It was to take many years for God to heal me but I think I've caused confusion in the people who have known me through my Christian journey. Slowly, I was learning to listen, but most of all, I was coming into a prayer life which was becoming my focus. It became my point of communication and the thing that was holding me in strength amidst people who doubted what had happened in me and who questioned the genuineness of my growing relationship with Christ. My total dependency was now firmly in Christ.

Although I have struggled with literacy all my life, I began to read more. The Bible excited me and I thirsted for more understanding of what was taking place. I became focused on the Word and started to respond to it as Christ gave me more understanding. I think this must have been very difficult for people who had known me many years, fellow Christians who perhaps couldn't understand my journey at this point. It had a detrimental effect on my relationships within the church I was in. I had not yet learned how to handle negative comments and only wanted to hear positive speech. I began to experience the love of God and was aware that in relationship with fellow Christians you would get along with some better than others. But I had no wisdom at that time in handling these challenges and so rejected anyone who disagreed with me. I really had a lot of growing to do but was blind to this at the time. I was beginning to experience a lot of physical pain and shared this with members of the church as the pain was unbearable at times. This pain increased over months at different times. It was suggested that it was psychological. My final decision to move to another church was at the point when one of my closest friends came to the house and threw a book down on the table. He said, "Accept that you're mentally ill!" and walked out. I was very distressed at this and I believe other members of the church also thought I was in denial.

So I moved to a new local church after prayer, now knowing that it was the Holy Spirit who led me there. Within the first year of being there, I was taken to hospital in agonising pain. Scans of my abdomen were taken and there was great confusion amongst the specialists. However, after about a week, three consultants visited me on the ward and told me they could find no reason for my pain and that I would be discharged in the next hour. I pleaded with them not to send me home as the pain was immense. They walked out of the ward and I can remember praying for help from God. Within two or three minutes of that prayer, they returned saying, "Mr Savory, you're going to have an operation tomorrow morning and you're first on the list! We can't see any reason for your pain but there are three theatres available and you will go into one of them, even if it is the heart theatre." This was about five o'clock that evening. I felt the most enormous relief and a big thankfulness to God for answered prayer. It was during my recovery period, as I was searching for answers about my situation that one doctor stated, "Truth is everything to you Gordon." I knew that my source was God and not the medical profession.

Next morning, I was offered a pre-med tablet which I refused. I can remember them saying, "You really should have it," but I said "No" as I so appreciated having a clear mind now that I was no longer under psychotic medication. But, slowly, I was beginning to believe I had cancer. I could think of no other explanation for the pain. The porters arrived to take me down to theatre and I began to pray quietly. As we entered the theatre, I was placed on the operating table.

I remember saying to God, "If this is to be my last moment on this earth, I truly give my life to You." I knew His love. All I can remember was the needle entering the back of my hand. The next thing I knew, I was waking up and feeling as though I had been kicked in the chest by a mule. Then, one of the theatre staff who had operated on me said he was really sorry. Straight away I thought he was going to say I had cancer. But he passed me a tube with thirty-two small gall stones in it and said, "We got it wrong." I then fell asleep. On waking, I was returned to the ward with the tube of gall stones still in my hand. I wasn't going to let those go! My thoughts for the next few hours were very mixed. I thought I would go back and tell all those who doubted the reality of my pain and set them straight. Once again my Heavenly Father spoke to me and said "no" in a silent way. In my heart he explained to me that He had been called a liar and placed on a cross as people had doubted Him, that He was the Messiah. Why should I be angry because of a few gall stones? I never did confront anyone. He really had humbled me and I had much learning to do. My journey in Christ really had started and I rejoice in that situation.

14

Going Deeper, Sowing Seeds

At this time, I was having difficulty with having left my previous local church. I missed it terribly, especially the friendships I had made. But what I was experiencing now was far deeper and more meaningful. Looking back, I can see that it was the Holy Spirit who had entered into my life but I was going through the baptism of fire. I was drawn to prayer more and more in my life, all the time asking for God's strength and help with understanding things. I would read and study the Bible all night. I would speak it out as I was learning it and be unaware of the time, I was fully absorbed. The pattern of my day would be to go to bed at ten o'clock at night and get up at twelve midnight to start studying. I was just being drawn deeper and deeper into prayer and the thrill of understanding God's written Word. I used to speak everything out that I was experiencing and learning. I had yet to understand that most of it was just for me but the excitement of the process overwhelmed me and I just couldn't keep silent! I'm afraid this pattern went on for quite a few years.

During my time at sea, there was a time when I was in Malta and I felt the need to pray. I was to learn, later in life, that the apostle Paul had been shipwrecked on this island. Soon after my healing, I bumped into a church friend, Matt, who prayed for me in the street. I recall telling him that I felt that my journey would not be dissimilar to the apostle Paul, but no way did I believe that I could claim to be at a spiritual level equal to Paul. I'd had a dream in which God had spoken to me and, as I was crying, He had told me that He would take all my pain and shame and use it for His glory. I felt at this time that what was happening within me was no longer containable. In 2006, I was baptised along with a few others from the church. I knew that I had received a christening sometime in my childhood. I'd also been baptised as a Jehovah's Witness, but this baptism was different in that I knew that I was giving myself as a complete sacrifice to Christ. My trust was in Him for all things. I wanted to live my life to the full in Christ and to be baptised was a natural part of that process − a public statement of my faith and obedience to Him. After baptism, I did experience temptation, but through the temptation, my Father gave me strength as I called on His name for help.

Shortly after my gall stones were removed I was diagnosed with irritable bowel syndrome. I was in a great deal of pain for the first year as I had much to learn about my dietary needs. One of the doctors told me I had no lining in my stomach or my small and large bowel. I was put under the monitoring of a hospital dietician and had to keep records of everything I ate. I saw the dietician on a regular basis for my progress to be monitored. After about nine months, it was established that my diet needed to be very restricted. I was always praying and hoping for complete healing for my dietary needs and every other need. Around this time, I attended an evening prayer meeting, after which a member of my present local church approached me. She shared a prophetic word with me saying that my healing would be slow. I had been told by medical experts that it could take around seven years before I began to experience improvements with my digestive health but there was also a chance of there being no recovery. The prophetic word has been confirmed by my experience; God has slowly brought healing emotionally and given me a healthy self-esteem. With regard to eating, it has been through stepping out in faith and being willing to take setbacks that I have come to my current acceptance of my diet restrictions. The only fluid intake I can have is water which I drink about four litres of each day. Food is just home-made bread and a little butter, fried trout, an occasional small amount of cheese and seventy per cent dark chocolate. I take the chocolate to help my digestive system function. I don't feel any hardship with the diet in itself but I feel sad that, in most situations, I miss out on the joy of sharing a meal with others. But I do enjoy cooking and sharing my gift of catering and hospitality. I still do experience difficulties with my digestive system and the amount of pain involved. I have also had a lot of adjusting to do regarding relationships and that too has been painful at times.

One of the ways I have handled this pain is to work on our allotment. In the early days after my breakthrough, I would go down to the allotment and work on it for as many as nine hours. I've always had an appreciation of nature and it gives me great happiness to watch things grow and has taught me patience. When you think that something has died, you shouldn't necessarily pull it up as a couple of weeks later it could start to flourish. This has been my experience on many occasions. I still work on the allotment, but for much less hours as the ground is more fertile and requires less attention. I love to share the products from the allotment as I acknowledge that only God makes all things grow and I don't like to waste anything. When giving away produce, people are often puzzled as to why I don't want money for it. But the way I look at it is that, from one seed, God has made food multiply. I'm only sharing what God has freely given me. God has opened doors for me through this giving, as it has allowed me to share my faith and the good things God has done for me. I often find the most effective way to share my faith is to tell of some funny incident that has happened on the allotment. For example, holes have to be dug but they are sometimes forgotten about and fallen into at a later date! In fact my wife had that experience and was not too chuffed with me afterwards. But after six years the fruit production on the allotment is very good. Many raspberries, lots of blackcurrants, apples, jostaberries, pears, strawberries and various vegetables have been harvested. I love to make pies and jams and give them away! I think people think I'm quite mad. How can you explain to someone, after being heavily sedated for years and years, the joy of being set free?

The physical strength I now have, though I'm a senior citizen, and the skills I've regained in the last seven years have blessed both me and others. I get the opportunity to pray with others when they share difficulties with me. Often in these relationships a lot of truth comes out of what has gone on in their lives. I pray silently inside as they are talking to me. What I find is that little by little, you can let your light shine and through perseverance, situations can change. I never take rejection as failure as sometimes it takes many years for a seed to grow; it's all in God's time and not ours.

15

Walk of Faith

One issue that I had to face after my breakthrough was that of debt and I had to acknowledge the situation I was in. This caused a great deal of guilt on my part as it was becoming painfully clear that my illness had brought a strain on my family both emotionally and financially. While I had been ill, I had made some bad choices in how I handled money. I had very little understanding of the value of money and the concepts of how to manage it effectively. I wanted to face these problems head on and take responsibility for doing something about it. I knew I couldn't cover every problem but there had to be a way through this situation with the Lord's help.

In late 2005, a new ministry began within my local church which helps people in debt situations. The ministry is called Christians Against Poverty and was started in Bradford in 1996 by John Kirkby. We approached the appropriate person for help and this was the beginning of a journey into financial freedom. It has been a difficult path for us, but we have stuck to the plan and are now debt free by God's grace! I can now value money in a healthy way and am better equipped to handle it wisely.

Another challenge for me since my recovery has been dealing with the stigma of mental illness. I have experienced people treating me as if I am unequipped to make sound decisions and handle responsibility. I appreciate that at one time, that was true of me, but I would like people to accept that my mental illness is now behind me.

One of the most difficult decisions to make and a pure step of faith was my choice to take the Foundation for Christian Service Course which ran for a year, starting in September 2006. The course involved attending classes on a Monday evening over three terms and completing assignments. After hearing that my local church was going to be running the course, I phoned to get more information. I knew the course would cost around a hundred pounds and, in the phone conversation, I gave information about my background and explained that I didn't have the finance to go ahead. To my astonishment, they said that was no problem, it was paid for! My reaction to that was quite emotional. I felt so blessed that God gave me this opportunity but still felt quite nervous and didn't fully believe that I could complete the course with my background.

During the course, I was drawn deeper and deeper into understanding Biblical truths and principles that would help me in my Christian journey. I did struggle immensely with the writing aspect of the course as there was regular coursework to be handed in for assessment. One of the tutors told me that I reminded her of her dad regarding my literal skills. Was it a good comment or bad I wonder?! But I know she loved her dad dearly and we would often laugh as I saw other students' neat writing and compared it with my squiggles. I was so enthusiastic with my answers to the coursework questions that I gave far longer answers than required. I was learning so much Biblical truth that I didn't want to hold back! However, I have grown in the understanding that a few words can be as effective as or more effective than lengthy explanations. While doing the course I was struggling with my physical weakness and pain and would sometimes have to leave the classroom to be sick. However, I did persevere through those difficulties and successfully completed the course in 2007. This achievement meant so much to me. I had persevered through pain and grown in my faith. I knew the Bible was true in every aspect and it contained prophetic words which we can allow to impact our lives, and the giver of understanding is God the Holy Spirit who reveals all things (John 16:5-16).

Looking back at my time of mental illness, I can appreciate how lonely and difficult life must have been for June and my daughters. For me, one of the hardest things about this is the knowledge that I can't recover those years. I can only hand this over in prayer to God, and I live because He lives. Greater is He that is in me than he that is in the world (1 John 4:4). My wife mourned over me during these years as she told me that she had said goodbye to the man she knew and I cried very much when she told me this. But I trust in Jesus, that amidst all things, He works for the good of those who love Him.

Shortly after my breakthrough, I was told that, statistically, there was only a twenty per cent chance that our marriage would survive. I instinctively knew that this wasn't God's will and I wouldn't allow what was said to influence my thinking. However, at low times in my journey, those words have come to my mind at which point I have said prayerfully, "Thy will be done." He really is a great Healer.

Christ's Invitation

No matter what situation you are in or what background you have, I encourage you to call upon Jesus Christ for your salvation and for any healing that you need. Jesus lived a perfect (righteous) life. By God's own plan, He was falsely accused and given over to be killed by crucifixion but was raised to life three days later. He died so we could be forgiven of our sins and He was wounded so we could be healed (1 Peter 2:24). When we are angry, it is a form of pain. Often this pain has been with us all our lives and yet we don't recognise it. It's only on the release of that pain, through a relationship with Jesus that we can obtain the joy of faith, hope and love. The gift that Jesus offers is open to all − don't miss out. It will mean you will have to forgive people for the wrongs they have done you but it will also mean that the wrongs you have done will be forgiven too (Matthew 6:14-15).

By taking the step of faith of receiving Christ's love and forgiveness, your life will become purposeful. You'll be able to be fulfilled because you will be entering into God's plan for your life. He can turn the most awful of circumstances into something good, something that brings Him glory. There was an immoral woman who came to Jesus and wiped His feet with her hair when he was a guest at a religious man's house. The man didn't show much appreciation of Jesus but the woman showed Him much love, knowing that He had forgiven her for her many sins (Luke 7:47).

Because I know I am released from my own sins, I have been able to write this testimony. Not long after I became a Christian, I studied a book called The

Purpose Driven Life by Rick Warren. This was one of the most enlightening and encouraging books I have read. Since reading it, I have come to know a purpose driven life for myself. Although I can't always see things clearly, I live by faith. When I look at life situations from a human perspective, I can't work it out, but through my relationship with God I am able to handle situations by His grace and take each day as it comes.

Below are some Scriptures I recommend you read to help you in responding to Christ. He is asking all people, everywhere to repent (change the way you think), turn from living a sinful life and live each day for God. God promises to give eternal life to all who trust and obey Christ.

John 3:16-17 | Mark 1:14-15 | Acts 2:36-39
Hebrews 11:1 | Matthew 7:24-29 | Matthew 11:28-30

Love

To share a love so good and fine,
To know a Master all divine,
That you might know that you are loved,
By the Saviour up above.

When confused, not thinking straight,
Let the Lord take the weight.
For I've learned in years gone by,
That he listens for your cry.

My child, my child, do not weep.
Come and sit at the Saviour's feet.
Oil I'll pour upon your head,
So you'll know that I'm not dead.
For I love each one of you.
Please accept that this is true.

By Gordon Savory

Acknowledgements

This story is an acknowledgement of the Lord Jesus Christ who has healed me and given me eyes to see His great power and His purpose in dying on the cross for us. I can now go forward on my journey with purpose.

I thank my dear wife June for her continual support, endurance and faithfulness through our relationship and the long period of my mental illness. You have shown great patience and love, right through into my time of recovery.

I thank Mark for the time and effort he has put into making this publication possible. Without his support and help to communicate my story and his patience in listening and allowing me time to handle my emotions, I could not have completed this project. Thanks also to Chris and Grace Smith for their kindness in proof-reading the book.

I thank River of Life Community Church, for accepting me for who I am and for welcoming, supporting and encouraging me through difficult times. Thanks to Pastor Paul Turner.

Lightning Source UK Ltd.
Milton Keynes UK
UKOW05f0758081013

218651UK00001B/33/P